LET US

Adore

HIM

TABLE OF

A NOTE FROM THE
Author

Observing Advent is relatively new to me. The closest I got was buying an Advent calendar and counting down the days until Christmas with my children. Our focus during those years was to enjoy the treat behind the little door and imagining all the gifts we would receive at Christmas. I guess this was because our Pentecostal tradition in South Africa shied away from anything that had the appearance of being too Catholic.

Only in the last ten years or so have I begun to appreciate the blessing of observing the four weeks of waiting, praying, and reflecting that typify Advent. This shift happened because my family moved to a new congregation where we read the Lectionary, lit the candles of hope, peace, joy, and love, and joined in corporate devotionals that started four Sundays before Christmas.

This new spiritual practice was invaluable to me. Advent became a season of anticipation during which I could savor the pleasure of the gift of Jesus. I could intentionally spend days meditating on the fact that God loved us so much, that he gave his Son to become a human being, like us, and to take our place. Through Jesus we are reconciled to the Father. Through the gift of Jesus, we are included in the family of God and share in the wonderful inheritance that belongs to Jesus. Meditating on hope, peace, joy, and love is like opening gift boxes where, even when we know what to expect, we cannot resist reveling in the wonderful grace and love revealed in the incarnate Christ.

My prayer is that this little devotional will be a source of blessing. May it remind us of all the good gifts that are ours in Christ Jesus. You may choose to read it by yourself or in a group. You may choose to answer the questions, or not. My only desire is that every day will lead you to greater intimacy with Jesus, by the power of his Holy Spirit, as you wait in him.

With much love,

Samantha Chambo

THE FIRST SUNDAY
OF ADVENT

Hope

NOVEMBER 27, 2022

SCRIPTURE

ROMANS 13:11–14

Besides this, you know what time it is, how it is now the moment for you to wake from sleep. For salvation is nearer to us now than when we became believers; the night is far gone, the day is near. Let us then lay aside the works of darkness and put on the armor of light.

ROMANS 13:11–12, NRSV

HYMN FOR THE WEEK

I care not today what the morrow may bring,
If shadow or sunshine or rain.
The Lord, I know, ruleth o'er everything,
And all of my worry is vain.

Living by faith in Jesus above,
Trusting, confiding in his great love;
Safe from all harm in his sheltering arm,
I'm living by faith and feel no alarm.[1]

---

1. James Wells (words), J. L. Heath (music), 1918, "Living by Faith," *Sing to the Lord: Hymnal* (Kansas City, MO: Lillenas Publishing Company, 1993), #566.

The first week of Advent in the Christian calendar marks the time when we prepare ourselves to commemorate the birth of Jesus, while also reminding ourselves that Jesus will come again to bring full and final salvation to humanity and the whole creation. During this period, we are waiting for the revelation of God.

This reminds me of dawn. Dawn is the time between day and night, when there is light outside but the sun is still below the horizon. It marks the transition between night and day, when the sky becomes brighter and the morning sun shyly heralds a brand-new day. This time is characterized by a beautiful blue sky and, depending on whether there are clouds, it may be blended with shades of bronze, orange, and yellow. It is an in-between time that erupts with hope. The obscurity of night and darkness fades to usher in a plethora of light and possibility.

The relationship between light and darkness is one of the apostle Paul's favorite metaphors to describe the life of the believing community. According to Paul, the coming of Christ as a human being ushered in a new era for humanity. It is one where the gloom, oppression, and darkness of sin are defeated and the light of salvation and liberty burst forth for all who believe. However, it is an in-between time. Although the first coming of Christ marked the start of this new time of life and hope, it will only be completed at the second coming—when Christ will destroy all the powers of sin, death, and darkness once and for all and the light of God will fill the earth like the waters cover the sea.

Paul thus admonishes believers to make sure that, even though there are still some traces of darkness in the world, they live as children of the light. This means that, as we eagerly await the arrival of Christ, we must be marked by the essence of light. We distance ourselves from the works of darkness, and we are characterized by the works of light. We strive to live in love and holiness, we oppose the darkness, and we make sure we are conduits of the light. All the while, we keep our eyes on the horizon as we actively wait for the full revelation of the desire of our hearts—Jesus Christ, our Lord and Savior.

BLESSING

Although you have not seen him, you love him; and even though you do not see him now, you believe in him and rejoice with an indescribable and glorious joy, for you are receiving the outcome of your faith, the salvation of your souls.

1 PETER 1:8-9, NRSV

QUESTIONS FOR DISCUSSION OR REFLECTION

1. Living at the intersection of time can be stressful because we are still confronted with the evidence of darkness. What are the traces of darkness that face the church in these days?

2. How have you seen the light of the love of Christ shining through in society?

3. How will you bring the light to your community?

The True Light

SCRIPTURE

JOHN 1:1–5, 9–14

In the beginning was the Word, and the Word was with God, and the Word was God. In him was life, and that life was the light of all mankind. The light shines in the darkness, and the darkness has not overcome it. The true light that gives light to everyone was coming into the world. The Word became flesh and made his dwelling among us. We have seen his glory, the glory of the one and only Son, who came from the Father, full of grace and truth.

JOHN 1:1, 4–5, 9, 14

The first chapter of the Gospel of John bursts forth with life, light, and power. Just as in Genesis 1, when God said, "Let there be light," so here John announces with boldness the coming of Jesus Christ, the Son of God, who was also present at the creation. He is the very Word of God, the power by which all things come into existence. What a bold, audacious thing to say.

According to John, Jesus, just like that first day of creation, came as light—and life, and glory. The very glory of God the Father! This was such an amazing, comforting, and empowering truth. This light is so forceful that the darkness has to recede in its presence. The light of Christ is proof that God is faithful, that he sent his Son to save, redeem, and restore his beloved creation.

This is not just a general salvation. It is specific and personalized to each and every one who believes and receives it. However, it is also vast enough to include the whole creation. The world in these days is plagued by illness, political unrest, natural disasters, and more. But into the chaos, God sent his Son to bring life, light, and order. On a personal level, we deal with loved ones who continue to live in self-destructive ways, illnesses that are chronic, financial problems that devastate our sense of self, and a host of other threats.

However, we can stand boldly in hope today. Our hope is not built on the shifting systems of this world but on Jesus Christ, the Son of the living God. In him are light, life, and the very glory of the Father. In him we have all we need. That is why we can choose once again to put our trust in him and rejoice in the fact that, through him, we are children of God. As children of God, we have hope. Our Father provided all we might need in the Son, Jesus Christ.

BLESSING

The Lord bless you and keep you; the Lord make his face shine on you and be gracious to you; the Lord turn his face toward you and give you peace.

NUMBERS 6:24–26

QUESTIONS FOR DISCUSSION OR REFLECTION

1. Reflect on the places where you have seen the light of Christ shine recently.

    _____

    _____

    _____

    _____

    _____

    _____

    _____

    _____

    _____

2. How do you need the power of Christ in your life right now?

    _____

    _____

    _____

    _____

    _____

    _____

    _____

    _____

    _____

    _____

    _____

The One Who Comes after Me

SCRIPTURE

JOHN 1:22–27

"I baptize with water," John replied, "but among you stands one you do not know. He is the one who comes after me, the straps of whose sandals I am not worthy to untie."

JOHN 1:26–27

I love the scene in the 2019 *Aladdin*, when Aladdin makes his flamboyant entrance with great flare and dramatics into the city of Agrabah. In this scene the genie goes out ahead of Aladdin and proclaims, "Make way for Prince Ali!" while the entourage dances and celebrates in brilliant colors. It is a spectacular announcement of a valiant prince who has come to impress the beautiful Princess Jasmine. This is the concept John is trying to convey when he calls himself a voice in the wilderness. He is the herald, the messenger who runs ahead of the great King to announce his imminent arrival.

John's message is one of hope. Just like in the times of Isaiah, he proclaims the coming of the Lord that will make a way in the wilderness, raise up every valley, and bring low the mountains and hills (Isaiah 40:3–4). John is announcing that the glory of the Lord will be revealed in Jesus Christ and that all the nations will see it. According to John, Jesus is the Lamb of God who is going to take away the sins of the whole world. Jesus is filled with the Spirit of God, and in turn, Jesus will pour out his Spirit on everyone. This fullness of God—all that God is and has and can do—is present in Jesus, and out of that fullness, we receive grace on top of grace (John 1:16).

The circumstances of our lives may lead to us crying out in pain, lament, and frustration. This is a natural response and, at times, a needed response. However, like John the Baptist, we also have a mandate to announce the hope that is in Jesus Christ. Such an announcement calls all people to look up and believe. Salvation is finally here. Healing and restoration are available. Forgiveness, redemption, and empowerment for life are provided in abundance. We can have hope, and we can breathe again.

BLESSING

May the God of hope fill you with all joy and peace as you trust in him, so that you may overflow with hope by the power of the Holy Spirit.

ROMANS 15:13

QUESTIONS FOR DISCUSSION OR REFLECTION

1. How does this reminder of our hope in Christ make you feel?

2. Whom do you know who will benefit from this announcement of hope?

3. How can you best proclaim the good news today?

I Saw You

SCRIPTURE

JOHN 1:43–51

"How do you know me?" Nathanael asked.
Jesus answered, "I saw you while you were still under
the fig tree before Philip called you."
Then Nathanael declared, "Rabbi, you are the Son of
God; you are the king of Israel."

JOHN 1:48–49

There is nothing better than feeling seen and heard. It feels good when people acknowledge who we are and what we contribute to the community. It feels good to be known. To know someone implies relationship; it denotes intimacy and mutuality. There are, of course, various levels of intimacy, and intimacy typically develops over time, as our knowledge of one another grows. But this is not the case with Christ. He knows us right now, and he loves us just as we are.

The story of the calling of Nathanael is a wonderful example of this personal knowledge that Christ has. Nathanael is sitting under a fig tree, reading from the books of the Law, when Philip comes running to him, all excited. Philip tells him they have found the Messiah and that Nathanael should come and see. Nathanael is skeptical. He wants to know if anything good really can come from Nazareth. Apparently, Nazareth does not have the best reputation.

However, something beautiful happens when Nathanael finally walks to Jesus. Jesus knows who he is! Jesus describes him as a true Israelite without any deceit. Nathanael is amazed—how does Jesus know him? When Jesus tells him how, Nathanael realizes that Jesus is no ordinary man. He is the Messiah—otherwise, how could he see Nathanael in this manner? Something good actually has come out of Nazareth.

I must admit, there are times when I get skeptical and times when I wonder, *Can anything good really come out of this particular situation?* Today I take courage. I have hope because I am known, I am heard, I am seen, and I am loved. My friend, just as Christ saw Nathanael under the fig tree, so he sees you today. And he is creating something good for your life. You are known and loved by our Savior. He is for you.

BLESSING

Oh, the depth of the riches of the wisdom and knowledge of God! How unsearchable his judgments, and his paths beyond tracing out! Who has known the mind of the Lord? Or who has been his counselor? Who has ever given to God, that God should repay them? For from him and through him and for him are all things. To him be the glory forever! Amen.

ROMANS 11:33-36

QUESTIONS FOR DISCUSSION OR REFLECTION

1. What do you want Christ to know about you today?

    _____

    _____

    _____

    _____

    _____

    _____

    _____

    _____

    _____

    _____

2. Spend time talking with him about it. Even though he knows everything, he loves it when we choose to open our hearts to him.

    _____

    _____

    _____

    _____

    _____

    _____

    _____

    _____

    _____

The Choice Wine

SCRIPTURE

JOHN 2:1–12

The master of the banquet tasted the water that had been turned into wine. He did not realize where it had come from, though the servants who had drawn the water knew. Then he called the bridegroom aside and said, "Everyone brings out the choice wine first and then the cheaper wine after the guests have had too much to drink; but you have saved the best till now." What Jesus did here in Cana of Galilee was the first of the signs through which he revealed his glory; and his disciples believed in him.

JOHN 2:9–11

What would this well-known story, where Jesus turns water into wine, look like if we approached it from the perspective of hope? The first thing that grabs my attention is the big empty jars. These big clay jars are used for purification rites, but now they stand in the courtyard empty, a vacancy, filled with the potential for the glory of God.

The second question on my mind is this: what is Mary hoping for? Why does she tell Jesus about the problem? Has her experience in raising Jesus given her the idea that he has the ability to resolve this humiliating problem?

Then there are the servants. They are given obscure instructions to carry almost 180 gallons of water to fill these big jars and then give the banquet emcee a drink from the filled jars. I am sure they are confused, but maybe they hope that Jesus has a plan they do not understand.

What is the result of the combination of all these elements—a mother's desire to see her son help save a family from embarrassment during a wedding; huge, empty stone jars; and servants who obey, even though the instructions are confusing? It is abundance—overflow. Those big jars are filled with 180 gallons of wine—much more than what they need! The second result is excellence, the wine superior to anything the banquet master has ever tasted. The most important outcome is glory. Jesus is marked by this miracle as the Son of God who came to save the world. Faith is the ultimate result; the disciples see this miracle and believe in Jesus.

BLESSING

Now to him who is able to do immeasurably more than all we ask or imagine, according to his power that is at work within us, to him be glory in the church and in Christ Jesus throughout all generations, for ever and ever! Amen.

EPHESIANS 3:20–21

QUESTIONS FOR DISCUSSION OR REFLECTION

1. What are the big empty places in your life right now?

   _____

   _____

   _____

   _____

   _____

2. What has your past experience with Jesus taught you that can encourage you?

   _____

   _____

   _____

   _____

   _____

   _____

   _____

3. How is Christ calling you to blind obedience? How will you respond?

   _____

   _____

   _____

   _____

   _____

   _____

   _____

FRIDAY, DECEMBER 2, 2022

I Will Raise It Again

SCRIPTURE

JOHN 2:13–25

In the temple courts he found people selling cattle, sheep and doves, and others sitting at tables exchanging money. So he made a whip out of cords, and drove all from the temple courts, both sheep and cattle; he scattered the coins of the money changers and overturned their tables. The Jews then responded to him, "What sign can you show us to prove your authority to do all this?" Jesus answered them, "Destroy this temple, and I will raise it again in three days."

JOHN 2:14–15, 18–19

Some of my favorite shows to watch are home renovation shows. I like watching how the builders put on their hard hats and goggles and take up their hammers and just start demolishing the inside of old, neglected homes. I imagine it must be cathartic. However, what I love best is to see the final outcome of the renovation project. I relish seeing a sad, old, ugly house transformed into a beautiful, inviting home. The demolition seems harsh, even violent, but the final outcome reveals that it was all worth it.

At first glance, Jesus's behavior in the temple seems out of control, violent, and even crazy. Why does he just burst into the temple with a whip and start driving people and animals out, turning over tables and shouting at them? I think this might be like the situation in the old house. The old religion, the old way of doing things, is not working. Instead of drawing the hearts of people closer to God, it has been creating the opposite effect. The situation has deteriorated so much that the temple—the holy dwelling place of the presence of God—is cluttered with people who are driven by greed and consumerism, defiling the holy temple, actually believing it is acceptable because the law does not forbid it. The old house has to go.

In its place God creates something new. When the Jewish leaders ask Jesus angrily what right he has to do this, he gives them a clue. He says, "Destroy this temple, and I will raise it again in three days." Jesus is, of course, referring to himself. He is the new temple, the very presence of God among his people. He is referring to his death and resurrection. Jesus is sharing a new hope. Finally, God has come to make his home with his people. Now it will no longer be about rules and regulations that people can manipulate to accommodate or justify their sins, but it will be about living in relationship with Jesus, the Son of God. This new way of worshiping will work because Jesus himself will enable us.

Sometimes the old needs to be destroyed for the wonderful new to come.

BLESSING

Finally, brothers and sisters, rejoice! Strive for full restoration, encourage one another, be of one mind, live in peace. And the God of love and peace will be with you.

2 CORINTHIANS 13:11

QUESTIONS FOR DISCUSSION OR REFLECTION

1. What are some of the strongholds that Jesus needs to demolish in your life?

2. What is the new thing that God wants to do in you, in your church, or in your community?

SCRIPTURE

JOHN 3:1–21

For God so loved the world that he gave his one and only Son, that whoever believes in him shall not perish but have eternal life.

JOHN 3:16

There is no greater source of hope than a newborn baby. The perfect little person is good, and filled to the brim with potential. She is still untouched by the fallenness of this world and has a capacity beyond imagination. He is pure hope.

In his conversation with Nicodemus, Jesus compares the change that needs to happen in people as being "born again." I don't blame Nicodemus for being confused. The concept is mind-boggling. Nicodemus asks how a person can return to the mother's womb. To his question I would add, how do I undo all the negative experiences, the rejection, betrayal, and other forms of suffering that have made me who I am today? How do I reshape the preset ways of thinking that have been ingrained into me with my mother's milk? How do I get rid of the dirt and grime that soiled me and left me feeling ashamed and unworthy? How can I be born again? Get a clean slate and start over?

Jesus gives the answer. He says that God loved us so much, that he sent his Son to die on the cross for us. The amazing source of hope is that Jesus did not come to condemn me for my current state. He came to save me. However, I do have to respond by believing in him. When I do, his light will come into my life, he will fill me with his Spirit, and he will drive out the darkness. This believing is ongoing, continuous. I have to continue to believe that I am made new in Jesus Christ and that all the old things are gone. I am born again.

As the new, born-again people of God, we—like newborn babies—can become a source of hope and light to the world. Our transformation is our testimony that God loves the world so much that he sent his Son. Our counter-cultural way of living, loving, and giving is like light in darkness. When we live as the new, transformed people of God, we proclaim the hope and restoration that can be found in Jesus Christ.

BLESSING

Therefore, if anyone is in Christ, the new creation has come: The old has gone, the new is here!

2 CORINTHIANS 5:17

1. What areas in your life are still a reflection of the old you?

2. How strongly do you believe in the ability of Jesus to change these dark spots?

3. How will you spread hope today?

THE SECOND SUNDAY
OF ADVENT

Peace

DECEMBER 4, 2022

SCRIPTURE

ROMANS 15:4–13

May the God who gives endurance and encouragement give you the same attitude of mind toward each other that Christ Jesus had, so that with one mind and one voice you may glorify the God and Father of our Lord Jesus Christ. Accept one another, then, just as Christ accepted you, in order to bring praise to God.

ROMANS 15:5–7

HYMN FOR THE WEEK

When peace like a river, attendeth my way,
When sorrows like sea billows roll,
Whatever my lot, thou hast taught me to say,
"It is well, it is well with my soul."
It is well with my soul;
It is well, it is well with my soul.[1]

---

1. Horatio G. Spafford (words, 1873), Philip P. Bliss (music, 1876), "It Is Well with My Soul," *Sing to the Lord,* #554.

My favorite present from a past Christmas season was a DNA kit my husband got for me. I discovered that I am 58 percent Sub-Saharan African, 27 percent European (mainly French and German), 10 percent Central & South Asian, and 3 percent East Asian and Native American. I am fascinated by this result because I cannot even begin to imagine that all these people from Africa, Europe, Asia, and even America, are represented in my person. I think it is pretty amazing.

The wonderful thing about DNA testing is that it challenges us to acknowledge that we are all *one humanity*. This is the same challenge that Paul gives to the church in Rome, which is made up of a mixture of Jewish and gentile believers. He says that even though they have been separate and at odds with each other in the past due to race and religion, now they are one in Christ Jesus. Thus, Paul prays for them that they will live in harmony with one another so they can bring glory to God with one voice.

Paul explains this idea even better in Ephesians: "For he himself is our peace, who has made the two groups one and has destroyed the barrier, the dividing wall of hostility" (2:14). What an amazing picture! Just like I am made up of a colorful array of DNA in my body, so all of us—people from every race, color, and background—are united in the body of Christ. We live in peace with one another because he is our peace. He broke down the walls that divide us and, through the cross, put to death hostility. Now we are free to love one another as brothers and sisters. In Christ, we are family.

Living in peace is more than merely avoiding conflict. It requires that we see one another in a new light. We share the DNA of Christ. We are real family, not simply a group

of people who share the same beliefs. We are blood rela-
tives, united by the blood of Christ. We share in the same
Holy Spirit, and we together bring glory to the Father by
living in the love of Christ.

BLESSING

May the God of hope fill you with all joy and peace as
you trust in him, so that you may overflow with hope by
the power of the Holy Spirit.

ROMANS 15:13

QUESTIONS FOR DISCUSSION OR REFLECTION

1. What are some of the dividing walls that separate us in the church today?

2. How can you actively seek to live in peace with your brothers and sisters in Christ?

Become less

SCRIPTURE

JOHN 3:22–36

He must become greater; I must become less.

JOHN 3:30

The most important aspect of peace in the Bible is relational—peace with God (Romans 5:1). The reason we need this peace, or reconciliation, is that we have broken our relationship with God by sinning. We needed a way to make up for our sins and to be made right with God.

Two of the most common ways to achieve this reconciliation in the Old Testament are through ritual washings and sacrifices. The Hebrews have many rules about washing and cleaning themselves before they eat and before they worship. Washing is a practice that not only cleans the physical body of the person, but as they practice it, they also acknowledge their need for inner cleansing. They need to be made clean from sin.

It's amazing how many times John refers to ritual washing in these verses. Jesus and his disciples are baptizing people (3:22), John and his disciples are also baptizing people (v. 23), and an argument starts between John's disciples and a man about ritual washing (v. 25). All of these references to baptism, water, and washing bring one thing to mind: how can people be made clean so they can have peace with God?

That John's disciples are not yet clean is obvious from their response to Jesus and his disciples. They are competitive because their aim is to see who gets the most people; they are envious and even a bit combative. However, John helps them by answering a question they have not asked: what is really important?

John points to Jesus. He helps them understand that Jesus is the most important person in their midst. *He* is the bridegroom, and all these people belong to him. They are not up for grabs, to belong to whichever leader is the most charismatic. Jesus came from heaven to make a way for us to have peace with God. This peace can only be ours when we continuously believe in Jesus, when we follow him, and when we allow ourselves to become smaller so Jesus can become our all in all. This, according to John, will turn away the wrath of God and ensure our eternal life.

Most of us reading this are already part of God's family. However, we do lose our peace at times because we forget what or who is important. We get caught up in the race for resources, recognition, and popularity. That is when we need to remember that Jesus is our only real source of peace with God.

BLESSING

Therefore, since we have been justified through faith, we have peace with God through our Lord Jesus Christ.

ROMANS 5:1

QUESTIONS FOR DISCUSSION OR REFLECTION

1. Are you at peace with God today?

2. What areas in your life do you need to decrease so that Christ may increase?

3. Do you see all humans as the bride of Christ? How would such a belief impact your relationships?

Talking with a Woman

SCRIPTURE

JOHN 4:1–42

When a Samaritan woman came to draw water, Jesus said to her, "Will you give me a drink?"
The Samaritan woman said to him, "You are a Jew and I am a Samaritan woman. How can you ask me for a drink?" (For Jews do not associate with Samaritans.)
Just then his disciples returned and were surprised to find him talking with a woman. But no one asked, "What do you want?" or "Why are you talking with her?"

JOHN 4:7, 9, 27

Maintaining peace with one another can be so challenging. There are many barriers that separate human beings. Ethnicity, gender, beliefs and ideologies, social status, and a host of other walls can appear insurmountable. However, in Jesus Christ, we can find a common place and find peace with each other.

The story of the woman at the well is saturated with all that we are supposed to separate. Ethnicity: Jesus is a

Jewish person talking to a Samaritan. The two do not get along. Gender: it is not respectable for a teacher of the law to speak with a woman in the manner Jesus does. Space: she worships on Jacob's mountain while Jesus worships at the temple. That Jesus chooses to sit there, wait for her, and speak to her is like a rhino crashing through a line of walls. It is astonishing.

Jesus finds common ground. Jacob is their common ancestor. Samaritans used to be part of the people of God. However, their ancestors chose to intermarry with gentiles, which led to them being cut off from the people of God. In Jesus Christ, they are welcomed back, they are still part of the chosen people of God, still recipients of the promise, even though they wandered off.

What was the promise? That God would pour out his Spirit on all people (Joel 2:28). This is the spring of living water that wells up to eternal life that Jesus is talking about in John 4:14. It is the blessed Holy Spirit who makes us part of the family of God, and family with one another. We all have the same Spirit, and we all share in the inheritance of Christ. All of us who believe in the Lord Jesus Christ and have received his Holy Spirit are one body, united in Christ Jesus.

Embracing the other—those who are different from us—is a powerful means to evangelize. Jesus reaches out to a lonely woman at a well in spite of all that is supposed to separate them. She finds joy and salvation, and she invites her people, the Samaritans, to come and listen to Jesus. Here once again Jesus does the unthinkable. He stays in a Samaritan village for two days. A Jewish teacher, choosing to receive hospitality from their sworn, sinful enemy? Can any good come from this? Apparently yes, because they all believe, and they host Jesus, but he becomes their host when he welcomes them into the newly imagined people of God.

It can be difficult to live in peace with people who are very different from ourselves. In Jesus Christ we can find common ground, where diversity is acknowledged, even celebrated, and unity is preserved because we do not seek to maintain peace by human means—we do it in the power of the Holy Spirit.

BLESSINGS

My prayer is not for them alone. I pray also for those who will believe in me through their message, that all of them may be one, Father, just as you are in me and I am in you. May they also be in us so that the world may believe that you have sent me.

JOHN 17:20–21

QUESTIONS FOR DISCUSSION OR REFLECTION

1. Are you living at peace with others from the household of faith?

2. What are some of the barriers that make it difficult to maintain the peace?

3. What are the common grounds that can draw you closer?

Jesus Saw Him

SCRIPTURE

JOHN 5:1–15

Here a great number of disabled people used to lie—the blind, the lame, the paralyzed.

One who was there had been an invalid for thirty-eight years. When Jesus saw him lying there and learned that he had been in this condition for a long time, he asked him, "Do you want to get well?"

Then Jesus said to him, "Get up! Pick up your mat and walk." At once the man was cured; he picked up his mat and walked. The day on which this took place was a Sabbath.

JOHN 5:3, 5–6, 8–9

Peace in the Bible means a lot more than just the absence of war, or feeling tranquil. The Hebrew word *shalom* is packed with meaning. It means wholeness, wealth, completeness. It is also more than just a state of being. It is action. That is why peace is linked with words like justice (or righteousness) and truth (Psalm 85:10; Zechariah 8:16–19).

Our story for today shows us the Prince of Peace in action, reaching out to people on the margin—those who are ill, broken, and rejected by society. This again is abnormal behavior for a teacher of the law because such exposure could defile him. But Jesus, in a range of actions, brings peace, wholeness, and justice to a man who has been held captive by paralysis for thirty-eight years.

First, we learn that Jesus *sees* him. This means Jesus takes the time to stop, to look, and to see the man's dire condition. Next, Jesus *learns*. The Greek word used here is *ginōskō*, which means "to know or understand." Jesus talks to him, gets to know him, listens to his story. Lastly, Jesus meets his need. He heals him, empowers him to take up his bed, and counsels him to stop sinning. Jesus takes radical action to bring the peace, wholeness, and restoration of God to this previously broken person.

Such radical acts of justice and compassion will always be met with opposition because they clash with the world's concept of peace. The world says, *follow the laws of convention, do not ruffle feathers, and please those in power—this is the way to peace.* However, that is not real peace, and Jesus knows it. The scribes and the Pharisees are unhappy that he has healed the man on the Sabbath, but Jesus is undeterred. He is the Prince of Peace, and his way is the authentic way to peace. It starts with stopping, seeing those on the margins, listening to them, and acting on their behalf.

As representatives of Jesus Christ, the Prince of Peace, we are called to be agents of his peace. This might not always have the appearance of peace because it might require that we speak up, get into conflict, or even find ourselves persecuted. In all of this, we follow the example of Jesus, who took time to stop, listen, learn, and act. There can be no real peace without justice (righteousness) and truth.

BLESSINGS

Blessed are the peacemakers, for they will be called children of God.

MATTHEW 5:9

QUESTIONS FOR DISCUSSION OR REFLECTION

1. How does this devotional reflection about Jesus's understanding of peace compare to your understanding of peace?

2. What actions are you called to do today to bring about the peace of Christ for others?

The Bread of God

SCRIPTURE

JOHN 6:25–59

Jesus said to them, "Very truly I tell you, it is not Moses who has given you the bread from heaven, but it is my Father who gives you the true bread from heaven. For the bread of God is the bread that comes down from heaven and gives life to the world."
"Sir," they said, "always give us this bread."
Jesus said to them, "Very truly I tell you, unless you eat the flesh of the Son of Man and drink his blood, you have no life in you. Whoever eats my flesh and drinks my blood has eternal life, and I will raise them up at the last day. For my flesh is real food and my blood is real drink. Whoever eats my flesh and drinks my blood remains in me, and I in them."

JOHN 6:32–34, 53–56

The life of an addict is a torturous one because the substance or addictive behavior always presents itself as the ultimate answer. The addiction pretends to be the perfect source of joy, peace, and love. It pretends to be utopia. This pretension is not limited to addicts; it is present in all of us, to some degree. We all have that one thing, person, or circumstance we perceive as a source of bliss, but deep down we also know it is our greatest source of torture. We can only tell the difference by the absence or presence of peace.

Such a pseudo heaven always comes with a struggle. When we get it, or when we indulge, it is immensely gratifying. However, the feeling is short-lived, followed by a gnawing sense of guilt, another craving, or a determination to get there again. This struggle is not always obvious; it's subversive, like the proverbial frog in the pot who does not know it is being boiled because the heat is increased very slowly. When it finally realizes what's happening, it's too late.

Jesus says his flesh is real food and his blood real drink. He is showing the Jews the error of their ways and pointing them in the right direction. He is the bread that came down from heaven. He is the only source of real peace, and joy, and love. But many people reject him because the teaching is too difficult (John 6:60, 66). They prefer the pseudo sources.

The answer for us today is to believe that Jesus is our only real source of peace, that only the Holy Spirit can give us real life. We might say, *I am a Christian, so I believe.* But do we really? What does our behavior reveal? Where do we turn to for joy and satisfaction? Where do we find peace and rest?

Such a belief requires letting go of our pseudo sources. We cannot hold onto Jesus *and* a pseudo—that will only create turmoil and, ultimately, combustion. A pseudo might appear innocent, harmless, even good. We can identify it when the Holy Spirit points it out, and when he does, we must agree, obey, and let it go. There can be no negotiations. Do you want an appearance of peace, or do you want the real thing?

Letting go is ongoing. We have to let go every day. Pseudos will always come back, charming, inviting, and logical. They will make a good case, offer an enticing warmth, and at the slightest opening, pounce! Thus, we turn to Jesus every day, we feast on his flesh and his blood every day. We treasure and cherish our wonderful peace because it is worth more than gold.

BLESSING

Beloved, I pray that all may go well with you and that you may be in good health, just as it is well with your soul.

3 JOHN 1:2, NRSV

QUESTIONS FOR DISCUSSION OR REFLECTION

1. Name that one thing that is a source of struggle for you.

_____

_____

_____

2. How can you surrender it to Christ today?

_____

_____

_____

_____

_____

_____

_____

_____

_____

_____

_____

_____

_____

_____

_____

_____

_____

_____

Even His Own Brothers

SCRIPTURE

JOHN 7:1-9

But when the Jewish Festival of Tabernacles was near, Jesus' brothers said to him, "Leave Galilee and go to Judea, so that your disciples there may see the works you do. No one who wants to become a public figure acts in secret. Since you are doing these things, show yourself to the world." For even his own brothers did not believe in him.

JOHN 7:2-5

Can you imagine what it must be like being the younger sibling of Jesus Christ? I can only imagine it was a bit like Joseph's brothers in Genesis 37. They know there is something special about him. They see the miracles he performs, and they were present when he turned water into wine (John 2). On the other hand, they also know he is just a person because they grew up with him, probably in the same room. They probably have also heard the stories about his birth. Their mom might have told them. In their hearts they know, amongst them all, he is the chosen one.

Their advice to go to the Feast of Tabernacles and show off his great powers reveals their frustration. I am sure they are aware the Jewish leaders will try to kill him, yet they still encourage him to go. So Jesus has to remind them that the world hates him. Is there a bit of the attitude of Joseph's brothers in them? Do they secretly imagine their lives might be better without him? On the other hand, his popularity probably has brought some fame to the family, and that could be why they want him to do miracles in public. That way they could at least benefit from his popularity.

Their behavior and words show us that they have preconceived ideas about what the Messiah will be like, how he is supposed to behave, and the benefits they should be able to reap from their connection with him. These preconceptions have deprived them of the full blessing of living in the presence of the Prince of Peace. Instead of enjoying the heavenly blessings his presence provides, they want the earthly glory.

Sometimes the only things standing between us and a life filled with the peace of Christ are our preconceived ideas and expectations. The apostle Paul is aware of this, so in Philippians 4:6–9 he urges prayer, which he says will combat anxiety and usher in "the peace of God, which transcends all understanding" (v. 7).

The way we think and expect can either be a barrier or a gateway to peace. We have to be intentional to set our minds on the things of Christ, not the things of the world.

BLESSING

Let the peace of Christ rule in your hearts, since as members of one body you were called to peace. And be thankful.

COLOSSIANS 3:15

QUESTIONS FOR DISCUSSION OR REFLECTION

1. What is currently stealing your peace, and how can you change your own beliefs or expectations to regain your peace?

_____

_____

_____

_____

_____

_____

_____

2. What, according to Philippians 4:4–9, are the mindsets that you need to adopt on your path to peace?

_____

_____

_____

_____

_____

_____

_____

Peace Be with You

SCRIPTURE

JOHN 20:19–23

Again Jesus said, "Peace be with you! As the Father has sent me, I am sending you." And with that he breathed on them and said, "Receive the Holy Spirit."

JOHN 20:21–22

The image that comes to mind when I think of peace is sitting in my comfortable chair, sipping some hot chocolate, and feeling at rest. However, as we have discovered, peace in the Bible is dynamic. It can come in moments of silence, but mostly it is found in a context of movement and activity. The disciples are all together, praying and worshiping, when Jesus appears in their presence. Jesus greets them by offering peace, but then he says he is sending them. Peace and mission go hand in hand.

We see the active nature of peace in many places in Scripture. In Matthew Jesus blesses peace*makers* (5:9); Luke talks about the "way of peace" (1:79, NRSV), which implies moving forward toward a goal. In Acts, the disciples preach peace in many different places (10:36). Peace mandates movement.

As we come to the end of this week, we reflect on all we have discussed concerning peace. But most importantly, we must decide whether we will go out and spread peace. The good news is that we don't have to do it on our own. We have the Spirit of Christ in us and with us, who is the ultimate source of peace. We follow in the footsteps of Christ on the way of peace. Just like him, we are willing to be blessed, broken, and given for those who are still far from God. Just like him, we are willing to speak, do, and go. We are willing to endure hardship and even persecution. We know that, because Christ paid the ultimate price for our peace, this is the least we can do.

BLESSING

Peace I leave with you; my peace I give you. I do not give to you as the world gives. Do not let your hearts be troubled and do not be afraid.

JOHN 14:27

QUESTIONS FOR DISCUSSION OR REFLECTION

1. Jesus has a unique calling on our lives. Where is he sending you today?

2. Think of one person who could do with the peace of Christ. Pray for that person.

3. How will you reach out to that person?

THE THIRD SUNDAY OF ADVENT

DECEMBER 11, 2022

SCRIPTURE

JAMES 5:7–10

Be patient, then, brothers and sisters, until the Lord's coming. See how the farmer waits for the land to yield its valuable crop, patiently waiting for the autumn and spring rains. You too, be patient and stand firm, because the Lord's coming is near.

JAMES 5:7–8

HYMN FOR THE WEEK

Joy to the world! The Lord is come
Let earth receive her King.
Let every heart prepare him room,
And heaven and nature sing,
And heaven and nature sing
And heaven, and heaven and nature sing[1]

---

1. Isaac Watts (words, 1719), George Frederick Handel (music, 1741), arr. by Lowell Mason (1848), "Joy to the World," *Sing to the Lord*, #173.

Waiting is difficult for me. I am an activator by nature, so I associate waiting with feelings of discomfort and frustration. This is why the idea of waiting in joy is so foreign to me. You might say, "What about waiting for something good to happen? Surely such anticipation can be a cause for joy!" I'm sure it is for most people, but not for me. I think the reason is that I struggle to believe the good thing will come. All the bad things that happened in my formative years have led to a situation where I assume the bad is just as possible as the good, so I generally wait in fear, anxious to see how it will pan out.

The good news today is that we can wait in joy during Advent because we know what will happen. We know that God, who is faithful, keeps his promises. He sent his Son because he loves us. We can wait in joyful anticipation.

The situation of the believers in Jerusalem, to whom James is writing, is a difficult one. The congregation is made up of Jewish Christians who fell on hard times after Peter left Jerusalem to plant more churches. We know there was a famine during this time, the believers suffered great poverty, and they were persecuted by the Jewish religious leaders. So James writes to encourage the believers and remind them of the teaching of Jesus. Most importantly, James reminds them that Jesus will return soon. James promises them that they will rejoice at the coming of Jesus, like farmers who rejoice with the coming of the rain.

James also warns that their attitude while waiting is important. They should not grumble and complain but should follow the examples of the prophets of old, who waited patiently for God to fulfill his promises. Believers should live humbly and avoid selfish ambition while they share the love of Christ in practical ways.

Beloveds, our current situation might be uncertain. However, today we can wait with joy because our God is faithful. We don't have to be anxious. We know he came through for us by sending his Son, Jesus. Our wait will be over soon. We know we will have our exuberant reunion with our Savior, so we are filled with inexpressible joy.

BLESSING

Blessed is the one who perseveres under trial because, having stood the test, that person will receive the crown of life that the Lord has promised to those who love him.

JAMES 1:12

QUESTIONS FOR DISCUSSION OR REFLECTION

1. How do you normally wait?

2. What brings you joy while you wait?

3. How can you encourage fellow believers as we all await the return of Jesus?

SCRIPTURE

ISAIAH 9:1-7

The people walking in darkness have seen a great light; on those living in the land of deep darkness a light has dawned. You have enlarged the nation and increased their joy; they rejoice before you as people rejoice at the harvest, as warriors rejoice when dividing the plunder.

ISAIAH 9:2-3

I love the Christmas season. It is rightly called a *festive* season because it is a time of joy and celebration. It is a sad fact, however, that this season is also a time of great stress for many people. We look back over the year and realize we did not accomplish all we hoped we would, or we have to deal with the fact that we don't have enough money. Some of us have to face Christmas without a loved one. There are many reasons Christmas is not always as joyful as it should be. So we turn to things that we think will make us feel better; maybe we max out our credit cards, or we return to relationships we know are destructive; some of us even turn to harmful substances and habits. We do it because we long for that sense of euphoria, for the joy that is supposed to be part of Christmas.

The joy that Isaiah describes is salvation joy. He says it is like a farmer who rejoices in a great harvest, and warriors over plunder—in both cases, the lives of those who rejoice depend on victory. Their relief is this: *wow, we are saved!* We can plant another year, we survived the battle. This joy is the result of knowing they are saved.

Isaiah writes to the people of Judah during a time of great darkness and gloom. The people have once again turned their backs on the Lord, and their sins of pride and rebellion result in the invasion of Israel and Judah by the Assyrians and Babylonians. They are in distress—some in captivity, others in exile, and the rest living under the oppressive rule of the invaders. Isaiah describes their situation as one of gloom and deep darkness. As Isaiah speaks to the people during this troubled time, he tells them they will suffer for a while longer but that their salvation is imminent because God is sending the Messiah, who will redeem the people of Israel. He prophesies concerning the people Israel, but he also looks much further and proclaims a great salvation that will be for the whole world, and this salvation will result in increased joy for all. Isaiah always links salvation with great joy.

Isaiah uses two common messianic symbols to explain the nature of this salvation. The first one is light. God will shine his light into the darkness. This light not only symbolizes God's blessing or justice but also refers to the very presence of God. This great light will be the manifest presence of the Almighty himself, stepping into the deep darkness of human beings to bring about a great salvation. This happened in the person of Jesus Christ. Jesus himself said, "I am the light of the world. Whoever follows me will never walk in darkness, but will have the light of life" (John 8:12). The second messianic symbol is the Davidic king. This Savior will be a descendant of David. However, unlike David and his other descendants, this King will get it right. He will not put his own sin and self-interest above the people. He will accomplish this salvation at great cost to himself. He will offer up his own life for the salvation of the people he loves.

This Christmas, our circumstances might not be ideal, but we can rejoice because we are saved! We rejoice because the wonderful light of Christ shines into our darkest places and because we are never alone. God has made his home among us. We are filled with great joy.

BLESSING

May the LORD answer you when you are in distress; may the name of the God of Jacob protect you. May he give you the desire of your heart and make all your plans succeed. May we shout for joy over your victory and lift up our banners in the name of our God. May the LORD grant all your requests.

PSALM 20:1, 4–5

QUESTIONS FOR DISCUSSION OR REFLECTION

1. Describe how you are feeling this year as you approach Christmas Day.

2. What brings you joy?

3. How can you add joy to the lives of others?

My Spirit Rejoices

SCRIPTURE

LUKE 1:46-56

And Mary said: "My soul glorifies the Lord and my spirit rejoices in God my Savior, for he has been mindful of the humble state of his servant. From now on all generations will call me blessed, for the Mighty One has done great things for me—holy is his name."

LUKE 1:46-49

The birth of a baby is generally an occasion for great rejoicing. I remember when I gave birth to my son, Emanuel. We were pastoring a local church at the time and living in the parsonage. What a time of celebration it was for the whole congregation. As soon as we got home our house was filled with people cooing and trying to determine whom he resembled. That was not difficult, of course—he was the spitting image of his dad. We were showered with gifts and money and many words of blessing. It was a time when the whole community could celebrate together.

The birth narratives in Luke's Gospel are no different. The stories are filled with the golden threads of joy and celebration. The baby John leaps for joy in Elizabeth's womb when Mary comes to visit, Mary bursts out in a song of Joy, Elizabeth's neighbors all come and rejoice with her at the birth of John the Baptist, and the angels tell the shepherds good news that brings them great joy while the angels glorify God in songs of praise. In fact, all through the narrative people respond to the good news by praising and glorifying God.

Mary's song gives us a few clues for her great joy. She rejoices in the fact that God chose her, a humble nobody, to participate in his great plan for salvation. Mary glorifies God because he has reversed the power systems of the world. He has rejected the rulers, the mighty, and the rich and instead has shown grace to the poor, weak, and humble.

She also rejoices for the inclusiveness of this salvation. Mary starts off by singing about how good God has been to her, but as she continues, she begins to rejoice in God's provision for the whole people of Israel—all of Abraham's descendants. This salvation is not just for a select few. Instead, all the nations will be blessed through Jesus. Everyone is invited to participate in the celebration.

Mary rejoices in the faithfulness of God to do all he promised. In his great love and mercy, he has not given up on his people. In Jesus Christ, God returned to his people to save and deliver them. He came to make all things right. During Advent we wait in joyful anticipation because in Christ there is a great reversal. All things are made right. We rejoice because he chooses us to be part of his family and part of his plan for the salvation of the world. We rejoice because we know our God is faithful. He always does what he promised. Praise his name.

BLESSING

Rejoice in the Lord always. I will say it again: Rejoice!
Let your gentleness be evident to all. The Lord is near.

PHILIPPIANS 4:4-5

QUESTIONS FOR DISCUSSION OR REFLECTION

1. How does it make you feel to know you have been chosen to be part of God's family?

2. How can you be part of God's intention to bring about a reversal in society?

3. How will you share this joy today?

Jesus, Full of Joy

SCRIPTURE

LUKE 10:21–24

At that time Jesus, full of joy through the Holy Spirit, said, "I praise you, Father, Lord of heaven and earth, because you have hidden these things from the wise and learned, and revealed them to little children. Yes, Father, for this is what you were pleased to do."

LUKE 10:21

The joy of Jesus captivates my imagination. It mystifies me to imagine that Jesus, the Son of God, can express such a human emotion. Even more thrilling is the fact that his joy could be in relation to us, simple humans. It reminds me of the time when both my children led worship in our local church. My daughter was the worship leader. She sang and played guitar with boldness and devotion. My son was the drummer. He played with such passion and surrender that it challenged the whole congregation to participate fully. My joy in seeing my children so passionate and committed to Christ was overwhelming. I found myself crying every

Sunday they played. I was thankful to see them serving Christ.

I think this must be the way Jesus felt. In the verses prior to today's scripture, he has sent out the seventy-two to preach the good news. Apparently, their mission is successful because they return full of joy and amazement. Even the demons flee when they command. At their report Jesus, filled with the Holy Spirit, starts to praise and thank the Father. He thanks the Father for choosing and revealing the good news to such simple people. He rejoices because they are like little children. They believe and accept the good news and have gone out in obedience to spread it to others.

Then Jesus turns to the disciples and speaks a blessing over them. He says they are blessed because God has chosen to reveal the secrets of heaven to them. The prophets of old all longed for this privilege, but they could only see it from afar. These disciples are privy to the greatest mystery ever: Jesus Christ, the Son of God, came as a human being to save and deliver all who believe in him.

The things that give Jesus joy are the same things that bring a parent joy. He rejoices when he sees his children believe in him. He bursts out in praise when we live out this faith and walk in all the blessings he has provided. He is even more ecstatic when we spread his love to those around us.

BLESSING

Then he turned to his disciples and said privately,
"Blessed are the eyes that see what you see. For I tell
you that many prophets and kings wanted to see what
you see but did not see it, and to hear what you hear
but did not hear it."

LUKE 10:23–24

QUESTIONS FOR DISCUSSION OR REFLECTION

1. How does it make you feel to know you can bring joy to Jesus?

    _____

    _____

    _____

    _____

    _____

    _____

    _____

    _____

    _____

    _____

2. How will you bring joy to Christ today?

    _____

    _____

    _____

    _____

    _____

    _____

    _____

    _____

    _____

    _____

With Great Joy

LUKE 24:50-53

When he had led them out to the vicinity of Bethany, he lifted up his hands and blessed them. While he was blessing them, he left them and was taken up into heaven. Then they worshiped him and returned to Jerusalem with great joy. And they stayed continually at the temple, praising God.

LUKE 24:50-53

The resurrection of Jesus overturns mourning and replaces it with joy. Luke, like a master weaver, entwines the golden threads of joy into the dreary aftermath of the crucifixion of Christ. We see the women, walking up to the grave, the heaviness of their hearts apparent in their slumped posture and muted conversations. However, their demeanor is about to have a radical change: the tomb was empty, and there are angels as bright as the sun proclaiming the resurrection of Jesus Christ.

The rest of the disciples are all sitting together in the small room of mourning, defeated. What are they supposed to do now that Jesus is gone? But then the women burst in, shouting that Jesus has risen. They jump up, filled with incredulity and hope, and rush to the grave to verify the women's story.

Two disciples on the road to Emmaus are talking about the awful crucifixion. Their faces are downcast. Then a stranger comes to walk with them. He eats with them, prays with them, and explains the deep things of God to them. His presence lifts their mourning and sets their hearts on fire. They cannot go to bed that night—they must rush back to Jerusalem to share the good news that Jesus has risen.

The disciples are all gathered together, talking about the amazing developments when Jesus appears in their midst, showing them his scars and reminding them of all he taught them, including his promised gift of the Holy Spirit. They are bewildered, but filled with much hope and joy. Jesus has come back to them.

On the Mount of Olives Jesus will leave them once more. But this time there is no room for mourning. This time they know that Jesus will never desert them. He is faithful, and he will send his Holy Spirit to be in them and with them. They return to Jerusalem, filled with joy.

BLESSING

Rejoice greatly, Daughter Zion! Shout, Daughter Jerusalem! See, your king comes to you, righteous and victorious, lowly and riding on a donkey, on a colt, the foal of a donkey.

ZECHARIAH 9:9

QUESTIONS FOR DISCUSSION OR REFLECTION

1. Where do you see the need for resurrection in the world around you?

    _____

    _____

    _____

    _____

    _____

    _____

2. How do you experience the presence of Jesus in your daily life?

    _____

    _____

    _____

    _____

    _____

    _____

    _____

    _____

    _____

    _____

    _____

    _____

    _____

Filled with Joy

ACTS 13:44-52

And the disciples were filled with joy and with the Holy Spirit.

ACTS 13:52

Did you know that joy is not a feeling but a gift? I am sure most mature Christians know this, but we cannot help but expect to *feel* it in order to believe we have joy. I personally am an emotionally sensitive person. My own emotions are larger than life, and I am sensitive to the emotions of others. This can be very disorienting, and can lead to me feeling helpless and ineffective in my daily life.

The Bible looks at joy from a totally different perspective. In the New Testament we see that joy is connected with the presence of the Holy Spirit (Luke 10:21; Acts 13:52; Romans 14:17). In Galatians we learn that joy is actually a fruit of the Holy Spirit, which has important implications for believers because it means that everyone who has the Holy Spirit has joy.

In our scripture for today we see the gift of joy in difficult circumstances. Paul has been preaching the good news to the Jews and gentiles. However, the Jewish leaders reject the good news, while other Jews and many gentiles receive it with joy. The Jewish leaders get jealous of Paul because so many believe in his message. They heap abuse on him (13:45) and persecute him and the believers who have chosen to accept this message.

We know, from the social context of the church in the first century, that the Christian believers were persecuted not only by Jewish leaders but also by their families and communities. These believers had stopped practicing many of the social norms that were culturally accepted during their time, which inevitably created resentment in their society and resulted in persecution. History teaches us that many Christians lost their lives due to persecution.

The confounding thing about this story from Acts is that, *in spite of* the hardship and persecution, the disciples are filled with joy and with the Holy Spirit. This joy is not just a feeling; it is the fruit of the Holy Spirit that they received when they believed in Jesus Christ. Difficulties cannot steal their joy. The implication of this scripture is that all of us can have joy. In the same way that we believe that Jesus is the Son of God, and received him as our Savior, we can believe that joy is the birthright of all believers and receive it in faith. This does not mean we will feel happy all the time or that things will always be good and easy, but we choose to receive the gift of joy on a daily basis. We bask in the joy of knowing that we are saved and filled with the Holy Spirit and that one day, when Christ returns, our joy will be complete.

BLESSING

Until now you have not asked for anything in my name.
Ask and you will receive, and your joy will be complete.

JOHN 16:24

QUESTIONS FOR DISCUSSION OR REFLECTION

1. What are some of the moments when you allowed your feelings instead of the Holy Spirit to guide you?

    _____

    _____

    _____

    _____

    _____

    _____

2. The Bible says joy is a fruit of the Holy Spirit. How is this evident in your life?

    _____

    _____

    _____

    _____

    _____

    _____

3. Think of someone who exemplifies joy in the Holy Spirit. What can you learn from this person?

    _____

    _____

    _____

    _____

    _____

    _____

Rejoice and Be Glad

SCRIPTURE

REVELATION 19:1–10

Then I heard what sounded like a great multitude, like the roar of rushing waters and like loud peals of thunder, shouting: "Hallelujah! For our Lord God Almighty reigns. Let us rejoice and be glad and give him glory! For the wedding of the Lamb has come, and his bride has made herself ready. Fine linen, bright and clean, was given her to wear." (Fine linen stands for the righteous acts of God's holy people.)

REVELATION 19:6–8

The book of Revelation has always been a source of great hope for me. My imagination is captivated by the description of the new heaven and the new earth. I love the stories about the new Jerusalem, the beautiful city of God—the city where there is no need for the sun or moon because the very presence of God will be the light for the people. Thinking about this glorious future is cause for joy, but Revelation is also an assurance of hope and joy for the present, even as we await the future joy. Revelation tells the story of humanity's sin and God's salvation in several different ways. It tells about how the kingdoms of this world rebel against God and refuse to repent. It explains that Jesus, the Lamb of God, will come and make all things right. He will judge the rebellious ones who refuse to believe and who persecute his people, and he will embrace and give life to those who have chosen to love him and care for his good creation.

Chapter 19 tells us the story of the great battle where the Lamb conquers the evil of this world and comes to take his bride, the church. The church is beautiful, dressed in white clothes and celebrating the victory of the Lamb. The scene is one of celebration, worship, and joy. The Lamb has defeated the powers of sin, evil, and death, and the church can rejoice forever in the loving presence of Christ.

John shares this vision of heaven to encourage the church and warn them to remain faithful to Christ. He wants to assure them that, even though they are going through difficult times, they can still have joy. They can rejoice in the knowledge that the Lamb has already overcome and that this means they too will conquer. John wants to remind them to hold on, not to give in to the powers and persuasions of this evil age. Their salvation is assured! Jesus is the Lamb of God who takes away the sins of the world.

Beloveds, today we can have joy because Christ is with us now, and we also look forward to the day when he will come to take us to our forever home in his brilliant presence.

BLESSING

And the God of all grace, who called you to his eternal glory in Christ, after you have suffered a little while, will himself restore you and make you strong, firm and steadfast. To him be the power for ever and ever. Amen.

1 PETER 5:10–11

QUESTIONS FOR DISCUSSION OR REFLECTION

1. How familiar are you with the book of Revelation? What are your favorite parts?

2. What are the implications of the victory of Christ for our lives today?

3. Revelation's many references to holiness remind us that holiness is important. How do you respond to such a reminder?

THE FOURTH SUNDAY OF ADVENT

Love

DECEMBER 18, 2022

SCRIPTURE

MATTHEW 1:18–25

"She will give birth to a son, and you are to give him the name Jesus, because he will save his people from their sins." All this took place to fulfill what the Lord had said through the prophet: "The virgin will conceive and give birth to a son, and they will call him Immanuel" (which means "God with us").

MATTHEW 1:21–23

HYMN FOR THE WEEK

Love divine, all loves excelling, joy of heaven to earth come down!
Fix in us thy humble dwelling; all thy faithful mercies crown.
Jesus, thou art all compassion; pure, unbounded love thou art.
Visit us with thy salvation; enter every trembling heart.
Breathe, O breathe thy loving spirit into every troubled breast!
Let us all in thee inherit; let us find that second rest.
Take away our bent to sinning; Alpha and Omega be.
End of faith, as its Beginning, set our hearts at liberty.[1]

1. Charles Wesley (words, 1747), John Zundel (music, 1870), "Love Divine, All Loves Excelling," *Sing to the Lord*, #507.

On this fourth Sunday of Advent, we are reminded of God's wonderful love. The promise of a Savior signifies that God is not willing to give up on us. He has provided all that is needed to reconcile us to himself.

When Joseph finds out that Mary is pregnant, he must feel many emotions. Anger, confusion, and disappointment are just a few that come to mind. This is definitely how I would react in his shoes. But, even though it must be a shock to him, he still decides to separate from her in private to save her from public humiliation. He has compassion on her. As he is contemplating his decision, the angel of the Lord appears to him and tells him that the baby is the Son of God and will save all people from their sins. Joseph believes the angel and chooses to stay with Mary and raise the baby as his own.

The angel reminds Joseph of the prophecies of old. The Messiah will be called Immanuel because, in him, God in gracious and faithful love will return to his people to save them from their sins. God loves us so much that he sent his Son to draw us back to himself. In Jesus Christ we are enabled to live in a loving relationship with our Father.

There is a song I used to love singing as a teenager. It was "Stubborn Love," by Kathy Troccoli. The chorus references God's "stubborn love that never lets go of me" and God's "perfect love embracing the worst in me." I loved this song because I was always aware of how I failed God. I loved Jesus, and I wanted to serve him, but I always found ways to get in trouble. One of my greatest fears was that God would give up on me. But he never did. Every time I confessed my sins, he forgave me. He restored me. He loved me!

This does not mean we are supposed to live a roller-coaster life, going in and out of faith all the time, although it is true that our faith can have seasons of ebbing and flowing. But God does not give up on us. His love draws us back to him, and his love also enables us to stay committed and faithful to him. I used to follow in fear—fear of punishment, fear of failure, fear of lack—but when I began to follow in love, following Christ became easy. I believed and accepted that Christ loved me and is eternally committed to me, and that enabled me to love him back and live in loving commitment to him. He is Immanuel—God with us.

BLESSING

Who shall separate us from the love of Christ? Shall trouble or hardship or persecution or famine or nakedness or danger or sword? No, in all these things we are more than conquerors through him who loved us. For I am convinced that neither death nor life, neither angels nor demons, neither the present nor the future, nor any powers, neither height nor depth, nor anything else in all creation, will be able to separate us from the love of God that is in Christ Jesus our Lord.

ROMANS 8:35, 37–39

QUESTIONS FOR DISCUSSION OR REFLECTION

1. How have you seen God's steadfast love in your life thus far? Write down a list to remind you of his love.

2. What is the Holy Spirit saying to you today?

SCRIPTURE

HOSEA 11:1-11

Oh, how can I give you up, Israel? How can I let you go? How can I destroy you like Admah or demolish you like Zeboiim? My heart is torn within me, and my compassion overflows. No, I will not unleash my fierce anger. I will not completely destroy Israel, for I am God and not a mere mortal. I am the Holy One living among you, and I will not come to destroy.

HOSEA 11:8-9, NLT

Don't you just love weddings? I remember my wedding day—my nerves, my excitement, how beautiful I felt, and how handsome my groom looked. It is probably the only day in my life when I really felt like a princess. I felt like a heroine in a love story.

I find it so amazing that God compares his relationship with us to that of a marriage covenant. And when we talk about "covenant," we refer to more than just a legal transaction. It is a relationship of love, mutual fidelity, and intimacy.

In Hosea, God uses the metaphor of marriage to depict the covenant relationship between God and us as God's bride. The story is a bit strange. God tells the prophet Hosea to go and marry a woman, Gomer, who will be adulterous and will even prostitute herself. It appears Hosea must take care of her illegitimate children as well. God tells Hosea to marry Gomer in order to reveal how much our infidelity hurts God, but also to show that God will always remain faithful to his covenant with us.

The people during the time of Hosea are religious and prosperous. However, they are worshiping other gods alongside the true God even though they made a covenant with God at Sinai to remain faithful to him alone. They know God made them prosperous, but they praise their idols for all that is going well in their lives. However, even in all of this, we see God as a devoted husband who is steadfast in his love, devotion, and faithfulness.

This story also reveals God's nature. God is not satisfied with empty religious expressions. He wants to be intimate with us. All the times he tells Hosea to take his wife back point to all the times God receives us back after we go looking for love in other places. It shows God's amazing restraint—that he does not give us what we deserve but chooses to pardon and restore us.

The story of Hosea and Gomer teaches us about God's ethical righteousness and judgment. Being in a right relationship with God leads to right behavior. God condemns wrong behavior. During Christmas, we remember that God loved us so much that he gave his Son to restore us to covenant relationship with himself.

BLESSINGS

Let us rejoice and be glad and give him glory! For the wedding of the Lamb has come, and his bride has made herself ready. Fine linen, bright and clean, was given her to wear. (Fine linen stands for the righteous acts of God's holy people.)

REVELATION 19:7–8

QUESTIONS FOR DISCUSSION OR REFLECTION

1. What parts of the story of Hosea and Gomer captivate your
    attention? This might be an indicator of God pointing out
    something in our relationship with him.

    _____

    _____

    _____

    _____

    _____

    _____

    _____

    _____

2. How will you respond to Christ's invitation to covenant faith-
    fulness today?

    _____

    _____

    _____

    _____

    _____

    _____

    _____

    _____

    _____

TUESDAY, DECEMBER 20, 2022

Great Love

SCRIPTURE

LUKE 7:36–50

*Therefore, I tell you, her many sins have been forgiven—
as her great love has shown. But whoever has been
forgiven little loves little.*

LUKE 7:47

In this last week of Advent, we reflect on the generosity of
God toward us, and we respond in like manner. I have always
focused on the woman when I read this story in Luke.
It is a story of a sinful woman who receives forgiveness
from Jesus and anoints his feet with expensive oil. This
woman's heart is filled with such love and gratitude that
she walks into a formal dinner uninvited, to show Jesus
just how grateful she is. She weeps over his feet and dries
them with her hair and then anoints him with expensive,
fragrant oil. This oil is worth a year's salary, but she does
not mind because she knows that she will never be able to
repay Jesus for all that he has done for her.

However, this story is also about Simon the Pharisee. Why
does Jesus go to Simon's house? The parable that Jesus
tells at dinner gives us an idea. Jesus tells the story for Simon's sake. The first debtor, forgiven little, is Simon. Jesus

compares Simon's condition to that of the sinful woman. He is a good man who has lived a good life. Jesus knows this. He knows all of Simon's good qualities. But Jesus tries to help Simon understand that being a good person is not enough. Simon needs more. He needs love in his heart, and Jesus hopes the example of this woman will help Simon to change, so Jesus goes to extra lengths to reach Simon.

Jesus proves to Simon that he is more than just a prophet by reading Simon's thoughts. He does not have to do this, but he knows the question in Simon's heart. Jesus shows Simon his sinful attitude. He compares Simon's lack of hospitality with the woman's excessively hospitable actions toward Jesus. These things that Jesus mentions (no water to wash his feet, no customary kiss, no oil on his head) are things that Jews normally did for any guest who arrived. The anointing was usually for VIPs. Simon has not done any of it. Jesus is saying to Simon, *Your behavior shows the condition of your heart. You might think you are the better person, but your loveless attitude reveals the opposite.* In contrast, the woman has given her very best— all she had—as a love offering. Jesus says her great love is evidence of the fact that she has been forgiven much.

BLESSINGS

However, as it is written, "What no eye has seen, what no ear has heard, and what no human mind has conceived—the things God has prepared for those who love him."

1 CORINTHIANS 2:9

QUESTIONS FOR DISCUSSION OR REFLECTION

1. Whom do you identify with most today? Simon or the sinful woman?

   _____

   _____

   _____

   _____

2. What is Christ challenging you to do?

   _____

   _____

   _____

   _____

   _____

   _____

   _____

   _____

   _____

   _____

   _____

   _____

   _____

   _____

   _____

Whoever lives in Love

SCRIPTURE

1 JOHN 4:7–21

Dear friends, let us love one another, for love comes from God. Everyone who loves has been born of God and knows God. Whoever does not love does not know God, because God is love. And so we know and rely on the love God has for us. God is love. Whoever lives in love lives in God, and God in them. We love because he first loved us. And he has given us this command: Anyone who loves God must also love their brother and sister.

1 JOHN 4:7–8, 16, 19, 21

One of my favorite things about Christmas is being home with family. In our family we normally gather in my mom's house. Everybody brings their signature dish, and there is normally a lot of loud talking, laughter, and eating. Even though all of us have gone on to set up our own homes, it is always such a joy to gather in my mom's home and revel in the love of our family.

In today's scripture, John tells us to live (or abide) in God because, when we abide in God, we abide in love. The Greek word used here for live/abide is *meno*, which can be translated "remain, stay, and reside." It can also mean to endure, or to continue in a given state. It means to make a home. It is hard for me to remain in Christ. I normally feel as if I am in Christ when I am in church or when I am praying, but what about the other times, when I am working and playing and living my normal life? What does it mean to abide in Christ in my day-to-day, rubber-hits-the-road life? What does it mean to live every minute of our lives in love?

We must remember that our Christian life is about love from start to finish. God, in his great love, included us in his family. First John 3:1 says: "See what great love the Father has lavished on us, that we should be called children of God!" Accepting Christ is like moving from one place to another. John explains it like moving from darkness to light. It is moving from our sin into the holiness of Christ. It is moving from rejection to love. We are in Christ because he loved us in the same way the Father loved him. Our job is to remain in his love. Jesus is our example of abiding. First John 2:6 says, "Whoever claims to live in him must live as Jesus did." Jesus lived in unity with the Father and the Holy Spirit, and he prayed we would live the same way. Jesus prayed "that all of them may be one, Father, just as you are in me and I am in you" (John 17:21).

Theologians refer to the relationship between the Father, Son, and Holy Spirit as *perichoresis*. Perichoresis conveys the understanding that the three exist in one another. The Latin translation depicts both movement and mutual rest, implying total openness to one another and mutual submission. The Father, Son, and Spirit are absolutely equal in this unity, and their activity in creation and salvation is an outflow of the unified purpose of the mutually indwelling God.

The wonderful truth about Christmas is that now, in Jesus Christ, we are included in this love relationship with the Father, Son, and Holy Spirit. This love is also manifested in how we live with one another—both fellow believers and those who do not know Christ. Living or abiding in love means walking in obedience, not sinning but knowing we can find forgiveness if we do sin. Abiding in love means releasing fear. It means living in victory "because the one who is in you is greater than the one who is in the world" (1 John 4:4).

BLESSING

If you abide in me, and my words abide in you, ask for whatever you wish, and it will be done for you. As the Father has loved me, so I have loved you; abide in my love.

JOHN 15:7, 9 (NRSV)

QUESTIONS FOR DISCUSSION OR REFLECTION

1. What are the things that pull you away from abiding in love?

2. What are the things that help you to abide in the love of Christ?

3. How will you be more intentional in abiding in the love of Christ?

SCRIPTURE

JOHN 21:15–19

When they had finished eating, Jesus said to Simon Peter, "Simon son of John, do you love me more than these?"
"Yes, Lord," he said, "you know that I love you."
Jesus said, "Feed my lambs."

JOHN 21:15

I've mentioned already that waiting is difficult for me. Sometimes it can get so stressful that I become inactive. I sit around twiddling my thumbs, waiting for the desired thing to happen. This is negative because there generally are lots of things I could be doing while I wait. This is also true of our waiting for Christ. Our waiting for the appearance of Christ is supposed to be active. We spread the love of Christ while we wait.

In our scripture for today, Jesus calls Peter to service. He is about to leave for the second time; soon he will ascend to heaven. Before he goes, he has an intimate conversation with Peter. Jesus wants to do two things: assure and restore Peter after Peter denied him three times, and commission him for the mission of the gospel. First Jesus reminds Peter of his denial by asking Peter three times if he loves Jesus. Peter denied Jesus three times; therefore, Jesus asks if he loves him three times to show Peter that he has forgiven him. It is never easy to be reminded of our weaknesses, and verse 17 tells us that Peter's feelings are hurt by this conversation. However, it is necessary for Peter—this way he will not return to his arrogance of the past but will live his life in total dependence on Christ.

Second, Jesus wanted to help Peter understand that love should be his main motivation for serving Christ. The work we do in the kingdom is a result of our loving relationship with Jesus. It is not because we are obligated but because we have a willing desire that is motivated by the love in our hearts. It is an outflow of remembering all the wonderful things Christ has done for us, and knowing we can never repay him for his great sacrifice.

Loving Jesus means that the things that are important to him become important to us. In Luke 4:18 Jesus talks about his mission to save and help all who are lost. Jesus lived his life healing and teaching. Jesus prayed for his disciples and for all who would believe because of them. We show our love by praying for the people God loves and serving them whenever we have an opportunity.

Loving Jesus requires sacrifice. During Christmas we remember that Jesus left his home in heaven, emptied himself of all his divine privileges, and ultimately sacrificed his life for us. During this holy season we offer everything to Jesus—all that we are, our time, talent, and money—as an offering of love.

BLESSING

I pray that out of his glorious riches he may strengthen you with power through his Spirit in your inner being, so that Christ may dwell in your hearts through faith. And I pray that you, being rooted and established in love, may have power, together with all the Lord's holy people, to grasp how wide and long and high and deep is the love of Christ, and to know this love that surpasses knowledge—that you may be filled to the measure of all the fullness of God.

EPHESIANS 3:16–19

QUESTIONS FOR DISCUSSION OR REFLECTION

1. What area of your life needs restoration today?

    _____

    _____

    _____

    _____

    _____

    _____

    _____

    _____

2. What is the work of love that Christ is laying on your heart?

    _____

    _____

    _____

    _____

    _____

    _____

    _____

    _____

    _____

    _____

    _____

    _____

    _____

Show Me Your Ways, Lord

SCRIPTURE

PSALM 25:1–10

Show me your ways, Lord, teach me your paths. Guide me in your truth and teach me, for you are God my Savior, and my hope is in you all day long.

PSALM 25:4–5

Psalm 25 is a beautiful psalm of desire. At first glance it seems as if the psalmist is asking God for wisdom, deliverance from enemies, guidance, and forgiveness of sins. But if we look closer, we see that he is actually asking to know God. He is asking for a personal revelation of the character of God. We see this in the many times he reminds God of his own character. The psalmist's biggest desire is to know God.

This reminds us of Moses's request in Exodus 33 and 34. It is a stressful time for Moses. The people have sinned against God by worshiping the golden calf, and Moses has broken the stone tablets in anger. To crown it all, God threatens not to accompany them to the promised land but to send an angel with them instead. So in chapter 34 Moses begs God to go with them, and to reveal himself to Moses. Here we see an intimate conversation between God and Moses. Moses makes the same request the psalmist makes in today's scripture: "If you are pleased with me, teach me your ways so I may know you and continue to find favor with you" (33:13). God responds by revealing God's character: "The LORD, the LORD, the compassionate and gracious God, slow to anger, abounding in love and faithfulness . . ." (34:6).

I am sure some of us have difficult situations as we approach this Christmas season. Others might be experiencing a time of peace and joy. Whatever our circumstances, may our deepest desire be to see and experience God, his steadfast love, and his unending faithfulness in and through our circumstances. May every need, every difficulty, every mishap, and every joy remind us to wait for the manifestation of Christ, who is our hope.

BLESSING

May the Lord make your love increase and overflow for each other and for everyone else, just as ours does for you. May he strengthen your hearts so that you will be blameless and holy in the presence of our God and Father when our Lord Jesus comes with all his holy ones.

1 THESSALONIANS 3:12-13

QUESTIONS FOR DISCUSSION OR REFLECTION

1. What are some of the difficult personal situations you have been facing this Advent season, and how is God revealing himself to you through these circumstances?

_____

_____

_____

_____

_____

_____

_____

2. What is your deepest desire as we approach the end of Advent and the beginning of the Christmas season?

_____

_____

_____

_____

_____

_____

_____

_____

_____

_____

Rooted and Established in Love

SCRIPTURE

EPHESIANS 3:14-21

I pray that out of his glorious riches he may strengthen you with power through his Spirit in your inner being, so that Christ may dwell in your hearts through faith. And I pray that you, being rooted and established in love, may have power, together with all the Lord's holy people, to grasp how wide and long and high and deep is the love of Christ, and to know this love that surpasses knowledge—that you may be filled to the measure of all the fullness of God.

EPHESIANS 3:16-19

It has been such a joy to wait with you. The family of Christ is beautiful and wonderful! Believers from all around the world can be united in the love of Christ as we sit together and as we meditate on the same scriptures and pray prayers of praise and thanksgiving and make petitions to our Father, who loves us. All this is made possible in Jesus Christ, who by the grace and love of God included us in his holy family.

This joy is what Paul is expressing in the book of Ephesians. In the first three chapters he praises God for the wonder that everyone is included in Christ—not just the Jewish nation. He rejoices in all the wonderful gifts and blessings that belong to those who are in Christ, and he prays beautiful prayers for all the believers.

Paul prays that we might be strengthened in our inner being by the power of the Holy Spirit, that we might be grounded in love, and that we together may know the great depth and breadth of the love of God in Christ Jesus. What Paul prays for is, of course, impossible. The love of God is beyond our comprehension, but Paul does give us some clues as to how we can have a better grasp of this amazing love: by the power of the Holy Spirit. It is not something we can figure out in our minds. It is the wonderful mystery of God, revealed in Jesus Christ. This mystery is only revealed to those who are in Christ, and who are filled with the Holy Spirit. We will only begin to comprehend this love as we pray and worship and open ourselves up to the Holy Spirit.

Paul also says we will understand it together with all of God's people, which suggests that the way to understanding this love is through the church of Christ. As we live, worship, and serve together, we will collectively begin to gain insight into the relentless love of God. We will be like trees whose roots go down deep and intertwine in the soil of Christ's love. We together will be rooted and strong and empowered to produce fruits that are exceedingly and abundantly more than we can even begin to imagine.

In the last three chapters of Ephesians, Paul offers some guidance on how the family of Christ is supposed to live. He calls us to live in truth, righteousness, self-control, mutual submission, and more. However, we must know that this holy new life is the fruit of being rooted and grounded in the wonderful love of Christ.

As we go into the celebrations of Christmas today, tomorrow, and beyond, I pray this prayer on us as the family of God, that we might be filled by the Holy Spirit, rooted and grounded in God's amazing love, and empowered to live fruitful lives to the glory of God the Father, God the Son, and God the Holy Spirit.

BLESSING

Peace to the brothers and sisters, and love with faith from God the Father and the Lord Jesus Christ. Grace to all who love our Lord Jesus Christ with an undying love.

EPHESIANS 6:23–24

QUESTIONS FOR DISCUSSION OR REFLECTION

1. What are your daily practices that help you to hear the voice of the Holy Spirit?

2. What are your weekly and monthly practices that help you unite with the family of God?

3. How will you include others in the love of God during the Christmas season?